CONTENTS

What are birds?

Birds are animals with wings, feathers and a beak. They are egg-laying animals. Most birds can fly.

class
a smaller group of living things; birds are in the class Aves (AY-veez)

phylum
(FIE-lum)
a group of living things with a similar body plan; birds belong to the phylum Chordata (kawr-DEY-tuh); mammals, reptiles and fish are also in this group

order
a group of living things that is smaller than a class; there are 23 orders of birds

kingdom
one of five very large groups into which all living things are placed; the two main kingdoms are plants and animals; birds belong to the animal kingdom

warm-blooded
having a body temperature that stays about the same all the time, no matter the surroundings; birds and mammals are warm-blooded

vertebrate
(VUR-tuh-brut)
an animal that has a backbone; birds are vertebrates

passerines
(PASS-er-inz)
the largest order of birds; more than half of all birds are passerines; all passerines have feet made for perching

species
(SPEE-sees)
a group of animals that are alike and can produce young with each other; there are about 10,000 species of birds

Part by part

Birds come in all sizes. But they share many of the same body parts.

nape
the back of a bird's neck

throat
the front of a bird's neck

wattle
a fleshy flap of skin that hangs from the neck of some birds; chicken wattles are usually bright red

breast
the part of a bird's body just below the throat

crown
the top
of a bird's
head

beak
a bird's
hard, usually
pointed mouthpart;
sometimes called
a bill

**field
marks**
the colours, spots
and lines on a bird's
body that help
tell one species
from another

wing
a body
part used for
flying or gliding;
birds have two
wings

Feathered friends

Birds are the only animals with feathers. Their feathers help them to fly and to keep warm. Colourful feathers may even help birds to find mates.

down
short, fluffy feathers; newly hatched chicks are covered with down

tail feathers
feathers that stick out from the end of a bird's body; these feathers help birds turn and stop when flying

moult
to shed old feathers so new ones can grow; ptarmigans moult twice a year; their feathers are white in winter and brown in summer

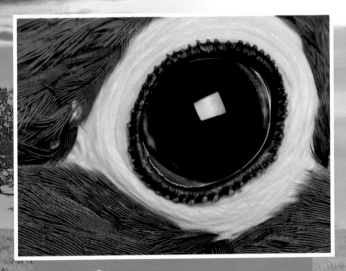

eyering

(I-ring): a narrow ring of feathers that circles a bird's eye; eyerings are different in colour from a bird's body

train

the long tail feathers that some male birds have; the peacock lifts his flashy train and shakes it to attract females

ruff

a ring of feathers circling a bird's neck; male sandpipers have a puffy ruff

crest

a group of feathers that grows from the top of a bird's head; northern royal

What birds do

crow
to make
a loud call;
roosters
crow

hover
(HUH-ver)
to float in the air
using wind currents or
wing movements; kestrels
hover while watching for
mice below; then they
swoop down to
make a kill

dance
some birds
do a fancy dance
to attract mates;
flamingoes dance
in large groups

preen
to clean
and straighten
feathers; preening
also helps remove
bugs and dust from
the feathers

stoop
the fast,
steep dive
of a bird of
prey

mimic
(MIM-ick)
to look or sound
like something else;
some parrots can
learn to mimic
human voices

roost
to settle down
for a night's rest;
birds do not roost
in the nests they build
for egg-laying; many
birds roost in trees
or bushes

swim
penguins
cannot fly, but
they are fast
swimmers

Raising a family

Birds work hard to survive. Many birds form pairs to make their work easier. These parent birds build nests for the eggs that the mother bird will lay.

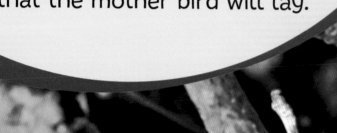

nest
a structure built by animals to hold their eggs; bird nests are usually made of sticks, leaves and mud; they're often lined with grass, feathers or spider silk

egg
birds lay eggs with hard shells; shell colours vary by species

clutch
a group of eggs that are all laid around the same time

incubate
(IN-kyoo-bate): to warm eggs by sitting on them so the chicks inside will hatch; male emperor penguins incubate their mate's egg for more than two months

brood patch
an area of bare skin on a bird's belly used to cover and keep eggs warm

hatch
to break out of an egg

chick
a newly hatched bird

egg tooth
a sharp bump at the end of a chick's beak; the egg tooth helps the chick to break out of the egg; after the chick hatches, its egg tooth disappears

brood
a family of young birds that hatch at about the same time

nestling
a young bird that's not old enough to leave the nest

regurgitate
(ri–GUR–ji–tayt): to spit up food that has already been swallowed; many birds regurgitate their food to feed their young

What's for dinner?

Some birds eat plants. Others eat animals. Let's see what's on the menu.

food chain

a series of living things in which each one eats the one before it; golden eagles are at the top of their food chain

predator

(PRED-uh-tur) an animal that hunts other animals for food

prey

(PRAY): an animal hunted by another animal for food; mice, smaller birds and rabbits are common prey for hawks

carnivore

(KAHR-nuh-vor): an animal that eats only meat; birds of prey, such as eagles and owls, are carnivores

seeds

seeds are a common food source for birds; blue jays eat sunflower seeds

nectar
(NEK-ter)
a sweet liquid found in flowers; hummingbirds use tube-like tongues to collect and drink nectar

insects
small animals with sectioned bodies and six legs; ants, beetles and other insects are one of the most common foods for wild birds

carrion
(KAR-ee-uhn)
the bodies of dead animals; vultures eat carrion

fish
pelicans swoop into the water to catch fish in their large throat pouches; other birds spear fish with their pointed beaks

brine shrimp
tiny shrimp that live in salty lakes and seas; flamingoes get their pink colour from eating brine shrimp

thing but nests

e bird nests are big and messy.
ers are as small as a walnut! But
irds make nests for the same
on. They want a safe place for
young to hatch and grow.

cupped nest
a nest shaped like a cup; made
of many different materials and
found in trees or bushes

ground nest
usually a cupped nest built right
on the ground; swans build
ground nests

mud nest
a nest built of mud and
sometimes animal droppings; the
sun dries the mud into hard clay

hanging nest
a long, sack-like nest that
hangs from a tree or place
above the ground; orioles
build hanging nests

cliff nest
a nest built on a high, rocky ledge; puffins build cliff nests

scrape nest
a type of ground nest made by making a shallow hole; killdeer build scrape nests

saliva nest
a nest made completely out of spit, or saliva; Asian swiftlets use their saliva to build nests on the sides of cliffs

cavity nest
a nest made in a tree hole or other empty space; hornbills make cavity nests inside hollow trees

burrow
a tunnel or hole in the ground made or used by an animal; burrowing owls find holes that rabbits or other animals have already dug

On the move

When the days turn cold, plants die off. Food is hard to find. Many birds fly to warmer parts of the world to find enough to eat. They return when the warm weather returns.

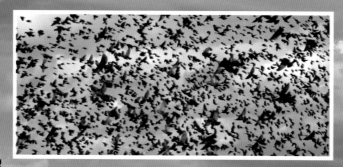

migrate

(MYE-grate): to move from one place to another when seasons change in order to find food or to mate; some birds may fly thousands of kilometres to reach their new homes

V-formation

(VEE for-MAY-shun): the V-shaped pattern that migrating geese make when they fly together; the shape helps the geese save energy and stay together; birds take turns flying at the front

navigate

(NAV-ih-gate): to find the way over a long distance; scientists do not fully understand how birds navigate to their winter homes every year

Canada goose
a common North American migrating bird; Canada geese fly north in spring and south in autumn

flyway
a route taken every year by large groups of migrating birds; there are eight main flyways around the world that cross land and often oceans too

fallout
the landing of large groups of birds when they are in trouble during migration; a fallout happens mainly when the birds are too tired, weak and hungry to fly any longer

route
(ROOT): a path taken to get from one place to another; many migrating birds, such as cranes, follow the same route year after year

resident
(REZ-uh-dent): a bird that does not migrate; resident birds can live in cold places as long as they have enough food; chickadees are resident birds

Water birds

Many birds live in and around water. They dive, glide and fish for food.

waterfowl
large water birds with rounded bills and webbed feet; swans are waterfowl; so are ducks and geese

duckling
a baby duck

webbed feet
feet with toes that are joined together by a flap of skin; webbed feet help water birds to swim and dive

waterproof
able to keep water out; the feathers of water birds are waterproof

wetlands

land that is full of water and water plants; birds such as egrets hide, hunt for food and nest in wetlands

drake

a male duck; mallard drakes have bright green heads to set them apart from females (brown heads)

shorebird

also called a wader; a bird that spends most of its time around water; storks nest on the shore and wade into the water to catch food

pelagic

(pel-AH-jik) animals that live on or in the open ocean and far from shore; pelagic birds, such as pelicans, come to land only to lay eggs and raise young

precocial

(pree-COH-shul) born already having feathers and open eyes; unlike other birds, water birds are precocial

Tropical birds

Tropical birds live in hot parts of the world. They are known for their bright, colourful feathers.

rainforest
a thick area of trees where rain falls almost every day; many tropical birds live in the rainforests of South America

toucan
(TOO-kan)
a brightly coloured tropical bird; toucans have short legs and a long, colourful beak

equator
(ih-KWAY-tur)
the imaginary line that circles Earth and divides the northern half from the southern half

Amazon Basin
the area of land in South America where the waters of the River Amazon drain; more than 1,500 bird species live in this area

tropical
having to
do with the hot,
humid part of the
world near the
equator called
the tropics

canopy
(KAN-uh-pee)
the treetops of
the highest trees in
a rainforest; hoatzins
live in the rainforest
canopy

plumage
(PLOO-mij)
another name for
a bird's feathers;
scarlet macaws have
bright red, blue and
gold plumage

parrot
a brightly
coloured tropical
bird with a large
beak; two of the
largest parrot species
are macaws and
cockatoos

macaws

23

Flightless birds

Most birds can fly. But about 40 species cannot. Birds that cannot fly often have a hard time escaping predators. Some species have died out.

elephant bird

an extinct bird that lived on only one island east of Africa; the elephant bird was the largest bird that ever lived; it weighed almost as much as a grizzly bear

extinct

(ek-STINGKT)
no longer living; an extinct animal is one that has died out, with no more of its kind on Earth; dodo birds (like the pictured models) probably became extinct in the late 1600s

ratites

(RA-tites)
a large group of birds that have no muscles to fly; ostriches are ratites

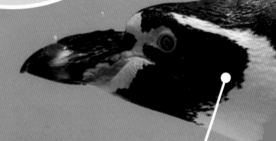

penguin

a type of flightless water bird; penguins have webbed feet and use their wings as flippers

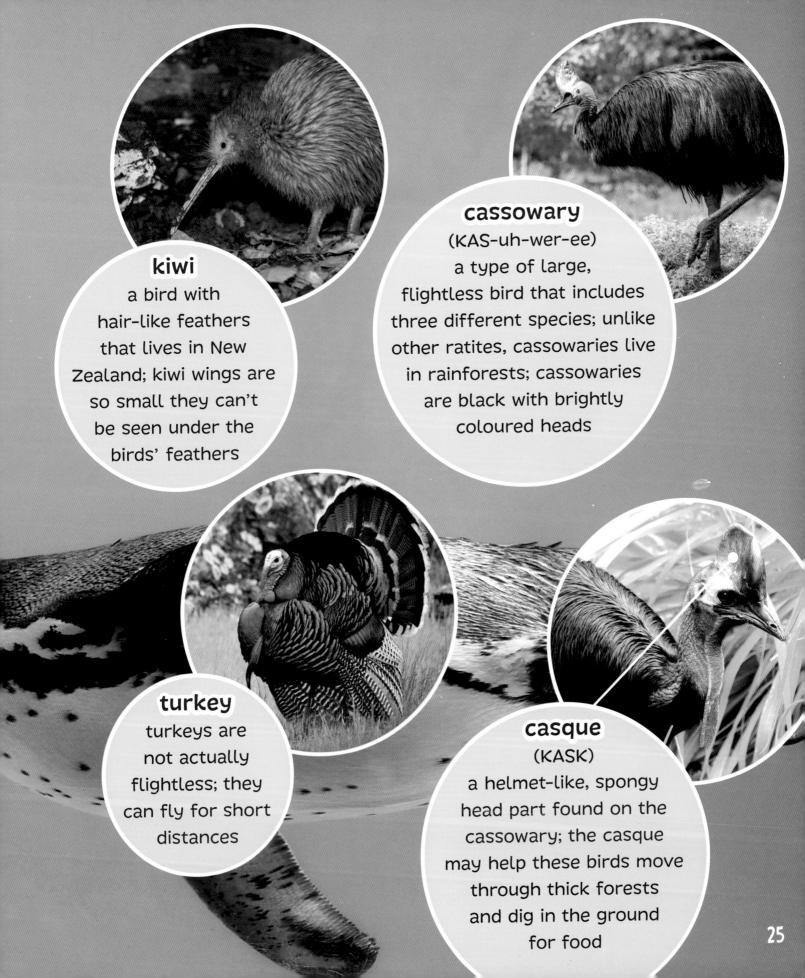

kiwi
a bird with hair-like feathers that lives in New Zealand; kiwi wings are so small they can't be seen under the birds' feathers

cassowary
(KAS-uh-wer-ee)
a type of large, flightless bird that includes three different species; unlike other ratites, cassowaries live in rainforests; cassowaries are black with brightly coloured heads

turkey
turkeys are not actually flightless; they can fly for short distances

casque
(KASK)
a helmet-like, spongy head part found on the cassowary; the casque may help these birds move through thick forests and dig in the ground for food

25

Birds of prey

Their eyesight is sharp. So are their hooked beaks and claws. Birds of prey are fierce hunters.

solitary
(SOL-ih-tayr-ee)
alone; most raptors live alone or in very small groups

raptor
another name for a bird of prey; raptors include owls, eagles and vultures; there are nearly 450 raptor species

wingspan
the measure of a bird's wings from the tip of one wing to the tip of the other; female raptors have longer wingspans than male raptors

nocturnal
(nok-TUR-nuhl)
active at night;
most owls rest
during the day and
hunt at night

owls
raptors
with big eyes and
round heads; special
feathers allow owls to
fly without making
any sound

falcon

hawks
the group
name for raptors
that includes
eagles, falcons,
kites and osprey

talon
a sharp claw
on a bird of
prey; an osprey's
talons are curved
to catch fish

27

Birdwatching

Some birds make good pets. Others are fun to watch from a distance. Seeing birds fly can give people a feeling of freedom. Their beautiful songs bring people joy.

binoculars
(buh-NOK-yuh-lerz)
a tool for seeing faraway things up close; birdwatchers use binoculars to study birds they can't get close to

dawn chorus
(DAWN KOR-us)
a group of many different birds all singing together just before the sun comes up; scientists aren't sure why birds sing at dawn and then go quiet

hobby
an activity done for fun; birdwatching is a hobby many people enjoy

birdhouse

a house made by people for birds to nest in; bluebirds like small, narrow houses with a little hole at the top

songbird

a bird known for the special songlike calls it makes; almost half of all birds are songbirds

warble

to sing softly in sounds that keep changing; the yellow warbler has a high-pitched warbling song

birdbath

a shallow dish for birds to bathe in; people often set up birdbaths in their garden

Fun facts

A **group of geese** is called a gaggle.

The fastest bird in the world is the **peregrine falcon**. It can dive-bomb faster than 322 kilometres (200 miles) per hour.

When **puffins** fly, their wings flap about 400 times per minute.

Ostriches reach running speeds of up to 72 km (45 miles) per hour.

The **harpy eagle** lives in the rainforests of Central and South America. To help catch prey, its claws can grow as large as a grizzly bear's.

The **southern cassowary** lives in Australia. It's known as the most dangerous bird in the world. When afraid, these birds go into attack mode. Sometimes they kill even large mammals like dogs.

Chickens are the closest living relatives to *Tyrannosaurus rex.*

Horned coots build their own islands in shallow water. They gather pebbles together and drop them in one place in the water over and over until an island forms. Then they cover it with plants. They make their nests on the islands.

FIND OUT MORE

Bird Watcher (Eyewitness Activities), David Burnie (DK, 2015)

Birds (Fact Cat Animals), Izzi Howell (Wayland, 2016)

The Great Nature Hunt: Birds, Cath Senker (Franklin Watts, 2016)

Why Do Birds Have Feathers? (Wildlife Wonders), Pat Jacobs (Franklin Watts, 2016)

WEBSITES

animals.nationalgeographic.com/animals/birds
Lots of information and photographs of birds.

www.rspb.org.uk/kids-and-schools/kids-and-families/kids/
Visit this website for facts about birds and games to play.

www.woodlandtrust.org.uk/naturedetectives/activities/2015/06/garden-birds-id/
A spotter activity sheet that you can download to help identify birds.